LIVES AND TIMES

# Florence Nightingale

## Rebecca Vickers

Heinemann
LIBRARY

**www.heinemann.co.uk.**
Visit our website to find out more information about **Heinemann Library** books

To order:

  Phone ++44 (0)1865 888066

Send a fax to ++44 (0)1865 314091

Visit the Heinemann Bookshop at www.heinemann.co.uk to browse our catalogue and order online.

First published in Great Britain by Heinemann Library,
Halley Court, Jordan Hill, Oxford OX2 8EJ,
a division of Reed Educational and Professional Publishing Ltd.
Heinemann is a registered trademark of Reed Educational & Professional Publishing Limited.

OXFORD MELBOURNE AUCKLAND JOHANNESBURG BLANTYRE
GABORONE IBADAN PORTSMOUTH NH (USA) CHICAGO

Designed by Visual Image
Illustrations by Sally Barton
Originated by Dot Gradations
Printed and bound in Hong Kong/China

ISBN 0 431 025169 (paperback)    ISBN 0 431 025150 (hardback)
05 04 03                         04 03 02
10 9 8 7 6 5                     10 9 8 7 6 5 4 3

**British Library Cataloguing in Publication Data**

Vickers, Rebecca
Florence Nightingale. – (Lives and Times)
1. Nightingale, Florence, 1820–1910 – Juvenile literature 2. Nurses – England – Biography – Juvenile literature
I. Title
610.7'3'092

**Acknowledgements**

The Publishers would like to thank the following for permission to reproduce photographs: Eye Ubiquitous: G Daniels p17; Hulton Getty: p16; Peter Newark's Historical Pictures: p18; Florence Nightingale Museum: pp19, 20, 21, 22, 23.

Cover photograph reproduced with permission of Hulton Getty.

Every effort has been made to contact copyright holders of any material reproduced in this book. Any omissions will be rectified in subsequent printings if notice is given to the Publisher.

Any words appearing in the text in bold, **like this**, are explained in the Glossary.

# Contents

# Early life

Florence Nightingale was born in 1820. Her parents were visiting Florence, in Italy. She was named after the city. Florence had one older sister called Parthenope. They lived with their parents.

Florence's parents were very rich. Like many rich girls of the time, Florence did not go to school. But she was a good **student**. Her father taught her foreign languages, history and mathematics.

# Nursing the sick

Florence's childhood was happy. As she grew older, Florence's parents thought she should find a rich young man and settle down as a wife and mother.

Florence realized that what she wanted was to nurse the sick. At the time, nurses were often **uneducated** old women. They were nothing like Florence! Her parents would not allow it!

# Wishing and hoping

Florence read all the books and **reports** she could about health and hospitals. She became an **expert** on the ways to keep people healthy and make them better when they became ill.

When she was 30, Florence went to Germany with some friends. She visited a nursing institute at Kaiserswerth. This was where she wanted to study!

# Nurse Nightingale

In 1851 Florence's parents finally allowed her to go to Kaiserswerth. She also went to Paris, in France, to work as a nurse. When Florence returned she worked at a hospital for sick women in London.

In 1854 Florence heard about the bad conditions for soldiers injured in the **Crimean War** between Britain and Russia. She had to do something.

# 'The Lady with the Lamp'

Florence gathered together supplies and a group of nurses. They travelled to Scutari Hospital in Turkey. Most of the injured soldiers were sent to Scutari.

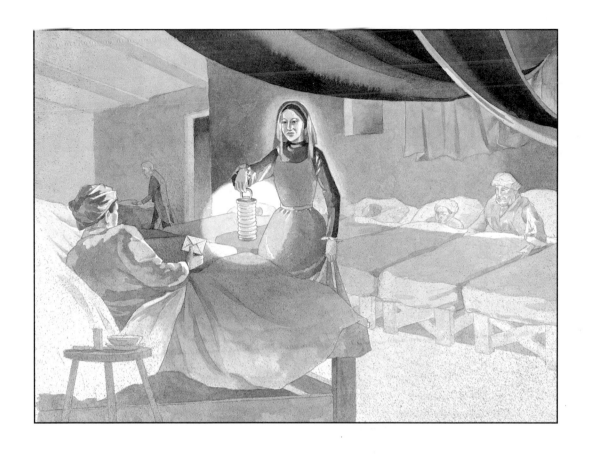

The men were happy to have cleaner **wards** and better food. They called Florence 'The Lady with the Lamp' because she walked around the hospital every night comforting **patients**.

# A national hero

When the war ended in 1856, Florence was famous. Even Queen Victoria wanted to meet her. In 1860 Florence set up the Nightingale School for Nurses in London.

Everyone wanted Florence's help and advice about hospitals and health. During her life nursing had become a **respected profession**. She died in 1910.

# Changes in nursing

Two hundred years ago there were no proper nurses to look after sick and injured people. Hospitals were often crowded, noisy and dirty places.

Today **patients** in hospitals are looked after by trained nurses. One reason for this is the hard work and **dedication** of Florence Nightingale.

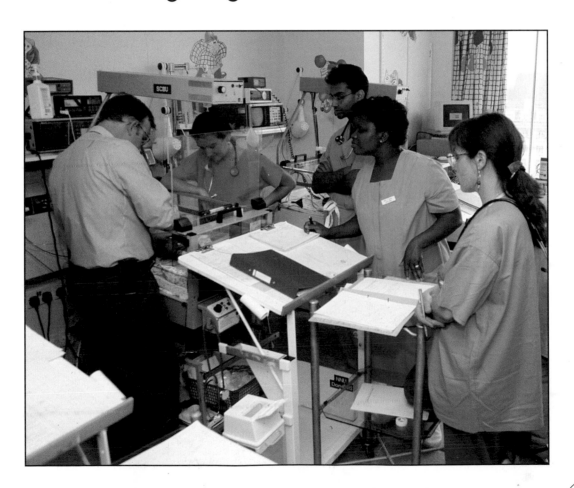

# Paintings

We can find out more about Florence Nightingale by looking at pictures. This painting shows Florence sitting with her sister Parthenope.

Here is a painting of Florence when she
was about 35 years old. She is in a **ward**
of the Barracks Hospital at Scutari.

# Photographs

Here is Florence with a group of nurses from the Nightingale School for Nurses at St Thomas's Hospital in London. It was the first time that nurses had been trained in a hospital.

Florence never stopped working, even though she was ill for nearly 50 years. This photograph shows her writing letters. For the last ten years of her life she was blind.

# Museums and artefacts

In London there is a Florence Nightingale Museum. It contains **artefacts** from Florence's life. Here are Florence's pen, ink, watch and writing box.

This is the lamp that Florence used to visit the sick soldiers in the hospital **wards**. She did this in Scutari during the **Crimean War**.

# Glossary

This glossary explains difficult words, and helps you to say words which may be hard to say.

**artefact** thing which people make and use. We can learn about the past by looking at old artefacts. You say *arty-fact*.

**Crimean War** (1854–1856) fought in an area on the Black Sea, in the south-east of what is now the Ukraine. You say *cry-me-un*.

**dedication** doing something with total love and devotion

**expert** someone who knows a lot about a particular subject

**patient** person who is being treated by a doctor for injuries or a disease

**profession** a job where there are special studies or exams to pass before you can do it

**report** information gathered together about a subject

**respected** someone or something that people think is important and valuable

**student** person who studies

**uneducated** someone who has not been to school

**ward** large, open room with many beds, found in hospitals

# Index

# Contents

Any words appearing in the text in bold, like this, are explained in the glossary.

# OUR PLANET: EARTH

Around 4.5 billion years ago a new star took shape from a giant cloud of gas and dust. This star was to become the Sun. Further away from the infant Sun giant gas **planets** formed. Closer in, smaller rocky worlds, including our own Earth, came into being.

## An oasis in space

The Earth is unique, like a beautiful blue-green ball when seen from space. It is an oasis of life in the vast emptiness of space. It is 150 million kilometres from the Sun, at just the right distance for it to be not too hot and not too cold. It is at just the right temperature for there to be liquid water. This is important because life as we know it needs water to survive. There may be unknown forms of life elsewhere in the **Universe** that do not need water, but there are none on our planet.

The Earth as seen from space.

To a traveller from a distant planet, Earth might seem a strange name for our world. Almost three-quarters of the Earth's surface is covered in water – most of it in the world's seas and oceans. Perhaps a better name for our world would be 'Ocean'!

4

## Sun dance

It might seem to you that you are sitting still as you read this but you are actually travelling very fast indeed. Far faster, in fact, than any aircraft. The Earth is spinning through space at over 100,000 kilometres per hour on a path round the Sun called its **orbit**. It takes just over 365 days for the Earth to go around the Sun once. This is what we mean by a year – the time it takes the Earth to complete one orbit around the Sun.

A tenth of the Earth's surface is permanently covered by ice. If all the ice on Earth were to melt at the same time, the level of the world's oceans would rise by about 55 metres.

### It's a fact – How far have you travelled?

In a year, the Earth travels nearly 940 million kilometres as it orbits the Sun. How far have you travelled since you were born?

### Try this – Empty spaces

**You need:** a basketball, a pea and a big open space

**What to do:** Put the basketball in the middle of the open space then take about a hundred paces from it. Put the pea here. You've just made a scale model of the Sun (the basketball) and the Earth (the pea)!

# DAY AND NIGHT

As the Earth follows its **orbit** around the Sun it is also spinning like a top. It turns around its **axis**, an imaginary line running through the centre of the Earth from the North Pole to the South Pole.

## All day long

It takes a little under 24 hours for the Earth to make one complete turn. One complete turn is called a day. As it turns, the spinning of the Earth points different areas of its surface towards the Sun. When the part of the Earth you are on is pointing towards the Sun it is daytime for you. For the people on the other side of the Earth, their side is pointing away from the Sun, so it is their night-time.

As the Earth continues to spin, your part of its surface gradually turns away from the Sun and it begins to get dark. At the same time, the part of the Earth that was in darkness is moving into the light. The Sun appears above the horizon and day breaks.

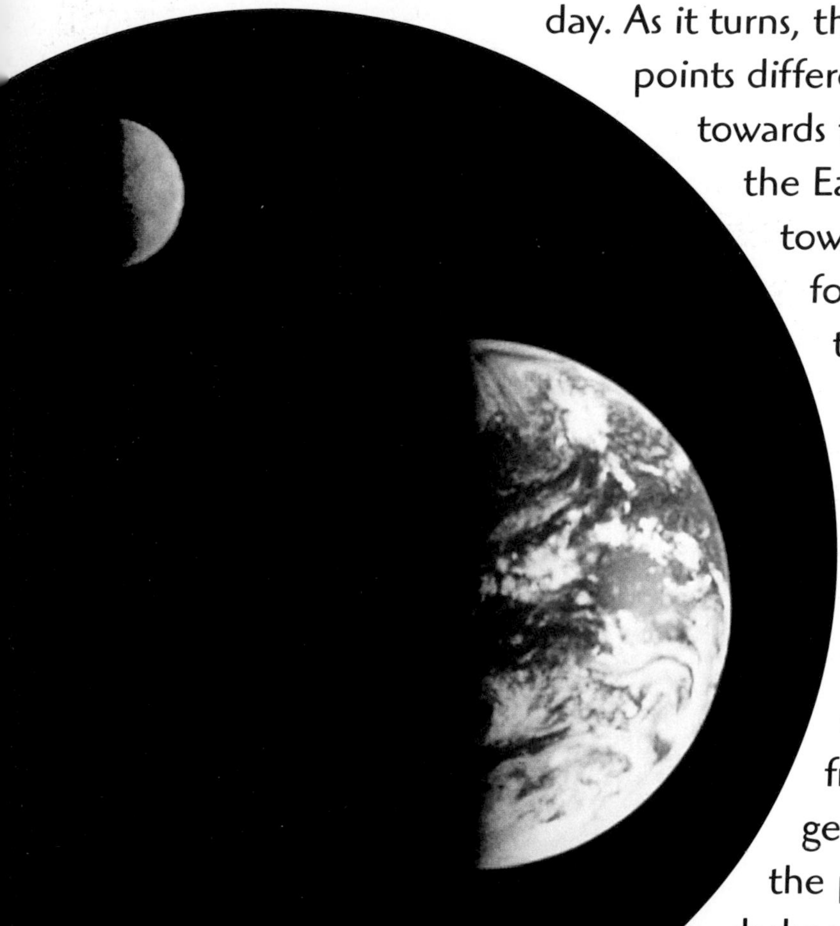

As the Earth and Moon spin different parts of their surfaces point towards the Sun.

## Turning stars

If you watch long enough at night you will see that the stars do not appear to stay in the same positions in the sky all night long. They look as if they follow circular paths around a point in the sky. This point is either the north or south **celestial pole** – an imaginary point in the sky above the actual Poles. Which one it is will depend on where you are on the Earth. It is only the spinning of the Earth that makes it look as if the stars are moving.

This long exposure photograph, taken over several hours, shows how the stars wheel around the night sky.

## It's a fact – As night turns to day

The Earth is spinning from west to east. This means that the Sun always appears to rise in the east and set in the west. This also means that places to the east of you start their day before you do, and places to the west of you end their day after you. The world is divided into 24 **time zones** to take account of differences.

## Try this – Making day and night

**You need:** a ball, a darkened room, a friend with a torch

**What to do:** Hold the ball with the tips of your fingers. Slowly turn it as your friend shines the torch on it. The torch 'Sun' brings 'day' to different areas of the ball as they turn towards it.

7

# THE SEASONS

The Earth is not quite upright as it spins through space on its **orbit** around the Sun. It is tilted over slightly on its **axis**, like an off-balance spinning top.

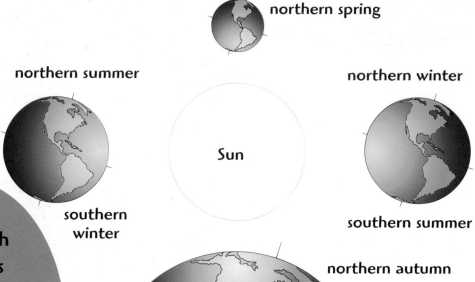

northern spring

northern summer

northern winter

Sun

southern winter

southern summer

northern autumn

As the earth travels in its orbit the tilt in its axis brings changing seasons to the north and south.

## Summer and winter

When the tilt of the Earth points the northern half of the world towards the Sun, the north gets more heat and light. This brings the long days of summer to the north. The longest day, midsummer day, or the summer **solstice**, is when the Sun appears at its highest in the sky. At this time in the southern half of the world, the opposite is true. The south points away from the Sun. Less heat and light reaches that part of the Earth and it is winter. The Sun does not climb high in the sky and the days are short.

After the summer solstice the Sun does not appear to climb so high in the north and the days begin to get shorter again. The Earth continues on its path around the Sun. As it does so the tilt begins to point the

December in Australia in the southern hemisphere is very different from December in Canada or London in the northern hemisphere.

## It's a fact –
## Long, cold nights

The polar regions are tilted so far away from the Sun in the winter that the Sun does not rise at all for three months of the year. In the summer it does not set for three months!

northern half away from the Sun. At the same time, the southern half is tilting towards the Sun. Days in the south begin to get longer at the same time as they are getting shorter in the north.

Half an orbit after the summer solstice the north has its winter solstice, or shortest day. That day the night is longest and the Sun stays low in the sky during the day. In the south, it is the summer solstice, and that part of the world has its longest day.

### Try this – Seasons diary

**You need:**   a notebook

**What to do:**   Start to keep a record of the changes you can see around you in the course of a year. Keep a note of the weather from day to day. Is it hot or cold? Is it wet or sunny? When do the leaves appear on the trees? When do the first flowers appear? Over the course of a year you can build up a valuable picture of the seasons in the place where you live.

# THE ACTIVE EARTH

The surface of the Earth is not formed in a single, solid piece, like the shell of an egg. Although we may not be able to feel it, the Earth's surface is actually broken into a number of massive slabs that are always on the move.

## Inside the Earth

The outermost part of the Earth is called the **crust**. It is made up of giant sections called **plates**. These plates float on a hot layer of rock about 2800 kilometres thick, called the **mantle**. Beneath the mantle is the **core**, the hottest part of the Earth. Heat from the core warms the bottom of the mantle and the hot rock gradually rises towards the surface. At the same time, cooler rock at the top of the mantle, which is denser and heavier than the hot rock, gradually sinks to the bottom. These movements produce slow **currents** in the mantle that carry the floating plates of the crust along like groceries on a supermarket checkout conveyor belt.

crust

mantle

core

Inside, the Earth is divided into three main zones – the core, the mantle and the outer crust.

## It's a fact – Ponderous plates

You won't see the Earth move because plates only move about as fast as your fingernails grow – around 5 centimetres a year!

10

In some places one plate slides beneath another, causing volcanoes and earthquakes.

sea level

plate

plate

melted rock rises

line of volcanoes

plate rock melts

## Bump and grind

When plates collide, one sometimes slides beneath the other, melting back into the mantle. The **molten** rock rises up and melts through the crust above, causing volcanoes and earthquakes. Sometimes when plates collide the force of the collision pushes and folds the crust into mountain ranges.

In some places, plates grind slowly past each other. Sometimes the plates stick together and then suddenly start to move again. The sudden jerk as they get moving once more is felt as an earthquake. Beneath the ocean, plates are moving apart. Molten rock rises up from the mantle to form new areas of sea floor between the plates.

### Try this – Moving currents

You should ask an adult to help with this.

**You need:** a heatproof glass dish, two wooden blocks, a small candle, some cooking oil and food colouring

**What to do:** Place the blocks on a level surface with the candle between them. Light the candle. Put some food colouring on the bottom of the dish then fill the dish halfway up with oil, being careful not to disturb the colour. Balance the dish carefully on the blocks. As the colouring heats up it will begin to rise through the oil just as hot rock rises up through the mantle. When it reaches the surface it will cool and begin to sink again.

# EARTHQUAKES

An earthquake is a sudden shaking of the Earth's **crust**. Thousands of earthquakes take place every day, but we feel only the biggest.

## Fractured Earth

The movement of the Earth's crust puts a great deal of strain on the rocks. If the rocks cannot move easily past each other a **fracture** suddenly opens in the rocks as they pass their breaking point. This releases a great deal of energy. It is a little like a rubber band that is stretched and stretched until it suddenly snaps.

Vibrations travel through the Earth at a high speed from the place where the fracture opens, which is called the **focus**. The point on the surface above the focus is called the **epicentre** and this is where most of the damage will occur.

## Feeling the force

A major earthquake can open up great cracks in the ground. Landslides and avalanches can cause further damage as the crust is shifted by the earthquake. Earthquakes may also form fountains which spray water, sand and mud.

fault

shock waves

epicentre

focus

Shockwaves spread from the focus of an earthquake deep beneath the surface.

In 1989 San Francisco was shaken by an earthquake. Another, perhaps stronger, quake could happen at any time.

## It's a fact – Tsunami terror

Earthquakes beneath the sea can cause powerful waves called **tsunamis**. These waves can race far across the deep oceans at up to 800 kilometres an hour. When the tsunami reaches land a wave 30 metres or more high can devastate lives and homes on the coastline.

Great damage can be done to buildings, bridges, roads and other constructions. Underground cables and gas pipes can be buckled and fractured by the earthquake, possibly causing fires to break out. Buildings that are well made from steel and reinforced concrete may be able to survive a powerful quake.

## Try this – Earthquake waves

**You need:**   a coiled spring and a friend

**What to do:**   You hold one end of the coiled spring while your friend holds the other. Push your end rapidly towards your friend. You should see a wave of compressed coils travel along the spring. Now shake the spring from side to side to make big waves. Earthquake vibrations travel through the Earth in both ways. It is the big up and down vibrations that do most damage.

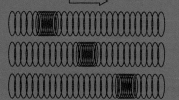

# VOLCANOES

Sometimes the **molten** rock beneath the Earth finds its way up through a weakness in the **crust** to the surface where it breaks out to form a volcano.

In 1991 Mount Pinatubo erupted in the Philippines, sending up huge clouds of ash and smoke.

## Fire on the mountain

The molten rock beneath the Earth's surface is called **magma**. Magma that pours out on to the surface is called **lava**. Large amounts of gas are trapped in the magma by the pressure of the tons of rock above it. When the magma comes near the surface, the pressure is eased and the gases escape. The great force of the expanding gases can break through weaknesses in the rock to reach the surface. This is the start of a volcanic **eruption**. The more gas there is to escape, the more powerful the eruption will be.

Great clouds of ash and dust may be carried high into the air by the rush of escaping gas. The hot ashes settle and form a cone around the gas hole. Lava pours from the hole and runs down the cone.

## Ring of fire

Most of the Earth's volcanoes are found in regions called volcanic belts. Volcanic belts lie along the edges of the **plates** that make up the Earth's crust. The biggest belt of active volcanoes, the 'Ring of Fire', surrounds the Pacific Ocean.

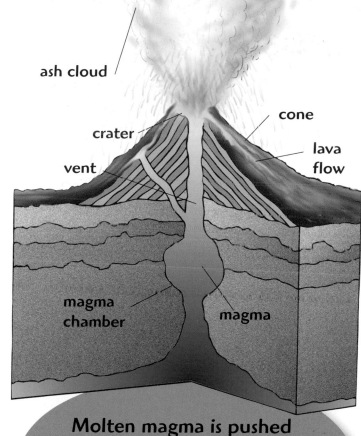

ash cloud

cone

crater

lava flow

vent

magma chamber

magma

**Molten magma is pushed up through vents in a volcano, pouring out onto the surface as lava.**

## It's a fact – Making a mountain!

On 20 February 1943, a farmer near Particutin, Mexico, saw smoke rising from his field. Within a few hours clouds of ash and smoke were pouring from a crack in the ground. Two days later lava started to flow out of the opening. By the time the new volcano stopped erupting in 1952, a cone 610 metres high had formed.

## Try this – Volcanic soup

You must ask an adult to help with this activity.

**You need:**     a pan of thick simmering soup and a pan of simmering water
**What to do:**   Look at the difference between a thick soup simmering and a pan of water simmering. The soup has large popping bubbles that may send soup splashing out of the pot. The water has fewer splashes. In the same way, some volcanoes erupt with great violence while others just pour out rivers of lava.

# MOUNTAINS

When two of the Earth's **plates** crash into each other, the **crust** is buckled and squeezed by the awesome forces at work. The rocks are pushed upwards to great heights to form a new chain of mountains.

## From sea floor to mountaintop

Because of the folding of the crust that takes place, mountains that form when plates collide are called **fold mountains**. Some of the highest mountain ranges in the world are fold mountains. About 45 million years ago the plate that carries India collided with the Asian plate. Rocks that were at the bottom of the ocean were pushed up to form what are now the Himalayas, which include the world's highest mountain, Mount Everest.

An expedition in the Himalayas, the world's highest mountain range.

## Blocks and blisters

Huge masses of rock can be shifted up or down along the lines of cracks or faults in the Earth's surface. These are called **block mountains**. The Sierra Nevada Mountains in California are block mountains. They have the steep sides that are typical of this type of mountain. The shifts in the crust that form the mountains can also give rise to earthquakes.

As we have seen, mountains can also be formed by volcanoes as a cone of **lava** and ash builds up around an opening in the crust. Hot **magma** beneath the surface can also blister the land above, pushing it up to form high, rounded **dome mountains**. The Auvergne region of France has a great many ancient dome mountains.

## It's a fact – Hidden heights

The highest mountain on land is Mount Everest at 8848 metres, but Mauna Kea, Hawaii, rises 10,205 metres from the ocean floor, making it the world's highest mountain.

The Sierra Nevada mountains of California are typical steep-sided block mountains.

## Try this – Make your own mountain range!

**You need:** three or four layers of modelling clay in different colours

**What to do:** Make some rock layers with the modelling clay, laying sheets one on top of the other. Make the layers as long as possible. Push the ends of the layers together. See how the layers fold up. Some may even fold right over so that layers that were underneath are now on top. This is often found in real mountains.

# ROCKS

The Earth's **crust** is made up of a number of different types of rock. There are three main kinds of rock: **igneous, sedimentary** and **metamorphic**.

## Igneous rock

Igneous rocks are rocks that have been **molten** and then cooled and become solid. Igneous means 'relating to fire'. Sometimes **magma** pushing slowly up through the crust cools and hardens before it reaches the surface. After millions of years, the crust above the cooled magma may be worn away and the mass of igneous rock can be seen. Magma that reaches the surface as **lava** also forms igneous rock when it becomes solid. Granite and basalt are the most common igneous rocks.

Over many millions of years the Earth's rocks are changed by a variety of forces beneath and on the surface.

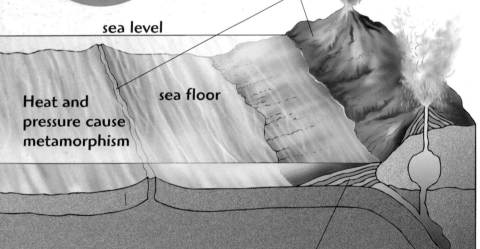

Igneous rocks form from cooled lava and magma

sea level

sea floor

Heat and pressure cause metamorphism

Sediments are deposited offshore

## Sedimentary rock

The rocks on the Earth's surface are continually being broken up by water, wind and ice.

## It's a fact – Skeleton rocks

Limestone is formed from the skeletons and shells of shellfish, coral and tiny plants that have sunk to the bottom of the sea over millions of years. Chalk is a limestone.

The fine rock pieces, called **sediment**, pile up at the mouths of rivers and on sea floors. As layer upon layer of sediment forms, the combined weight of the upper layers puts enormous pressure on the lower layers. Water is squeezed out from between the grains as they are pressed together to form a solid mass of rock called sedimentary rock. Sandstone is one type of sedimentary rock.

## Metamorphic rock

Magma pushing up through the crust can heat up and squeeze sedimentary or igneous rocks nearby. The moving crust can also put pressure on rocks. This heat and pressure may change these rocks into different forms. Limestone is changed to marble, for instance. Rocks transformed in this way are called metamorphic rocks.

A slate mine. Slate is a form of metamorphic rock often used in building.

## Try this – Make your own sandstone

**You need:** plaster of Paris, fine-grained sand, water and a clear plastic bottle

**What to do:** Cut the top half off the bottle and discard it. Mix the plaster of Paris and sand in the bottom of the bottle. Add some water and stir. The mixture should be easy to stir but not too runny. If you add too much water just make a small hole in the base of the bottle and let it run out. Leave the mixture to harden over night. Cut away the bottle (you may want to ask an adult to help with this) and remove your 'sandstone'.

# SOIL FORMATION

Over long stretches of time even solid rock can be broken down. Wind and water pound at the solid rock, heat and cold crack its surface and gradually the rock is worn away.

## Weathering

The breakdown of rock is called **weathering**. Temperature changes play a big part in this. As rock heats it expands and then shrinks again as it cools. This can begin to break up the rock as cracks form in the surface. If water gets into the cracks and then freezes, this pushes the cracks open even more.

## Erosion

The pieces of rock that fall off may not stay in the same place. Running water, moving ice in the form of **glaciers**, or the wind can transport the rock fragments far away from the original rock. This is called **erosion**. The rock fragments may bump and rub together as they are moved along, which breaks them down even further.

The Grand Canyon in the USA is the world's biggest river canyon. Eroded by the Colorado River, it is 1600 metres deep and up to 20 kilometres wide.

## From rock to soil

If you dig down deep enough beneath the soil you will eventually reach rock. The break up of rock through weathering is the first stage in the formation of soil. **Lichens** and mosses can gain a hold in the cracks of a weathered rock. They produce chemicals that eat into the surface of the rock to release the minerals they need to grow. These plants can also trap tiny particles in the cracks of the rock. Gradually over a period of perhaps thousands of years a layer of soil begins to build up and bigger plants take root. Tiny animals, spiders and insects, take up residence. **Bacteria** and **fungi** break down the wastes and the remains of animals and plants, and these further enrich the soil.

In a healthy patch of soil there is a thriving community of plants and animals all making their living directly or indirectly from the soil.

## It's a fact – Dig deep!

In warm, moist areas soils can be up to 5 metres deep, but in very cold and dry areas the soil may be only 1 centimetre deep.

### Try this – Ice cracking

**You need:** a ball of clay, some water, a plastic bag and a freezer

**What to do:** Wet the clay and put it into the plastic bag. Now put the bag in the freezer. Leave it overnight. Next day take a look at the ball. See how the ice that has formed has cracked and broken its surface.

# ATMOSPHERE AND CLIMATE

The **atmosphere** is like a protective blanket spread over the Earth. It keeps us warm by trapping heat from the Sun and shields us from **meteors**. It is the source of the air we breathe.

A section through the Earth's atmosphere. A big thundercloud can stretch from 2 to 15km through the atmosphere. The highest clouds form up to 90km up.

## Earth's blanket

The atmosphere stretches up from the Earth's surface, gradually getting thinner and thinner until it fades into space. Ninety-nine per cent of the atmosphere lies in the first 30 kilometres. The atmosphere is a mixture of gases, mainly nitrogen and oxygen. It is oxygen we breathe to stay alive.

All but the largest meteors (stray rocks flying through space) are burned up in the atmosphere if they enter it. The atmosphere lets sunlight in, but other rays more harmful to life, are filtered out.

10km — Cirrus

Anvil of cumulonimbus clouds

Cirrocumulus

Cumulonimbus

6km —

Altostratus

Altocumulus

Cumulus

2km —

Stratus

Stratocumulus

Sea level —

Nearly a third of the Earth's surface is covered by desert regions, where little rain falls. The Atacama Desert in Chile formed beside a mountain range which blocks rain-carrying clouds.

## What's the weather?

The lowest part of the atmosphere, up to about 10 kilometres, is where the weather happens. The air is heated by the Earth, which is warmed by the Sun. Warm air rises and cools causing winds and rains.

The weather changes from day to day. On some days the sun shines, on other days it rains. Over a long period of time, however, the weather can be seen to fall into repeating patterns. This is the **climate** of a region – the usual pattern of weather over a period of years.

### It's a fact – A skin of air
If the Earth was the size of an apple, the atmosphere would be no thicker than the skin!

### Try this – Miniature climates
**You need:** some fast-growing seeds, such as cress or mustard, small washed-out yoghurt pots, cotton wool or tissue paper

**What to do:** Fill the pots with loosely packed tissue paper or cotton wool and scatter some seeds on the top. Water one pot and put it in a warm, light place. Sprinkle it with water every day. This is your warm, damp climate. Put another pot where it will get as much direct sunlight as possible, but give it no water. This is the hot, dry climate. Where do your plants grow best?

# THE SUN

Without the Sun there would be no life on Earth. Almost all of the heat and light that life needs to survive on our **planet** comes from the Sun.

## Atomic fire

The Sun is a gigantic ball of hot gas nearly 1.4 million kilometres across. It is so massive that the material in the centre of the Sun has become very compressed. Everything in the **Universe** is made of tiny particles called **atoms**. In the centre of the Sun, and in other stars, the atoms smash into each other with such force that they fuse together. Huge amounts of energy are given off as this happens. In the Sun this takes the form of heat and light energy. The temperature at the centre of the Sun is incredibly high, about 14,000,000°C.

The Sun is an immense ball of hot gas, giving off light and heat in all directions.

## When day turns to night

When a total **eclipse** occurs it is as if night has fallen in the middle of the day. An eclipse of the Sun happens when the Moon moves between the Sun and Earth and casts a shadow over part of the Earth. Beneath the shadow, the Sun seems to disappear as the Moon moves in front of it.

When the Sun has been totally blocked a halo of bright gas is seen around the Sun. This is the **corona**, the Sun's atmosphere. The sky darkens and stars become visible even though it is the middle of the day. A total eclipse can last up to 7 minutes and 40 seconds, but they are normally much shorter.

We can only see eclipses because of a remarkable coincidence. The Sun is 400 times bigger than the Moon, but the Moon is 400 times closer, so they both appear to be the same size in the sky. This means that the disc of the Moon fits neatly over the disc of the Sun!

This multiple exposure photograph shows the Sun's disk being obscured by the Moon passing in front of it.

## It's a fact – The speed of light!

It takes light, travelling at about 300,000 kilometres per second, just over 8 minutes to travel the 150 million kilometres from the Sun to the Earth.

## Try this – Eclipsing

**You need:** a dinner plate, a coin and a friend

**What to do:** Ask your friend to stand a few metres away and hold the dinner plate up to represent the Sun. Now take the coin, which represents the Moon, in your hand and hold it up. Close one eye and line up the coin and the plate. Even though the coin is really much smaller, you can make it appear to cover up the plate, because the plate is further away.

# THE MOON

The brightest object in the night sky is the Moon. It is our closest companion in space, and the only world other than our own that people have visited.

## A rocky sphere

The Moon is a rocky sphere in space. It is less than a third of the size of the Earth and **orbits** it at a distance of around 384,000 kilometres. It takes just over 27 days for the Moon to travel once around the Earth. This is also the time it takes for the Moon to turn once on its **axis**. This means that the Moon always keeps the same side facing us.

The surface of the Moon is scarred by craters formed by meteor strikes many millions of years ago.

The surface of the Moon is covered by **craters**. Many of these were caused by **meteorites** striking the surface at high speed. The Moon has no **atmosphere** to protect it. Some are around 200 kilometres across – big enough to swallow up most of Belgium! Other craters may have been formed by volcanic activity.

## It's a fact – Permanent prints

Because there is no rain or wind on the Moon there is no **erosion**. The footprints left by the Apollo astronauts are still there nearly 30 years after the Moon landings.

## Phases of the Moon

The Moon gives off no light of its own. It shines by reflecting the light of the Sun. When the Moon is between the Earth and the Sun, the side of the Moon pointing towards us is in shadow and we cannot see it from Earth. This is the New Moon. Just after New Moon, a thin crescent appears on the eastern side of the Moon. Each night the crescent gets a bit bigger. Full Moon is when the whole face of the Moon is lit up by the Sun. After Full Moon the eastern half of the Moon begins to darken. Gradually it becomes a New Moon once more.

The Moon appears to go through phases as we only see the part of its surface that is lit by the Sun.

## Try this – Mirror Moon

**You need:** a flashlight, a round mirror, two friends to help

**What to do:** One person should be the Sun and hold the flashlight. This person should stand to one side and point the light towards the other two. The second person is the Earth and stands still. The third person is the Moon and holds the mirror against his or her chest. The Moon person moves slowly round the Earth person, facing the 'Earth' all the time. As the 'Moon' moves, the 'Earth' will see that sometimes the 'Sun' is reflected in the mirror and sometimes it is not, depending on their positions.

# OUR PLACE IN SPACE

The Earth is just one of nine **planets** travelling around the Sun. Millions of **asteroids**, **comets** and **meteoroids**, plus dust and gases all circle the Sun as well. The Sun and all this multitude of objects in **orbit** around it together make up the Solar System.

## The Solar System

The Sun is by far the biggest object in the Solar System. Ninety-nine per cent of the mass of the Solar System is contained in the Sun. Starting with the closest to the Sun, the nine planets are: Mercury, Venus, Earth, Mars, Jupiter, Saturn, Uranus, Neptune and Pluto. The Earth is an average-sized planet. Its diameter of 12,700 kilometres is three times that of tiny Pluto but less than a tenth that of the giant planet Jupiter.

Between Mars and Jupiter lies the Asteroid Belt, where most of these minor planets, the asteroids, are to be found. Beyond Pluto, far out towards the outer reaches of the Solar System, is the Oort Cloud, a vast cloud of comets left over from when the Sun and planets formed.

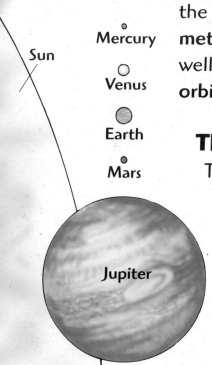

Sun

Mercury

Venus

Earth

Mars

Jupiter

Saturn

Uranus

Neptune

to

**The Sun's family of planets.**

### It's a fact – A far away star

It is almost impossible to imagine how vast the **Universe** is. If the whole Solar System was shrunk to the size of the city of Paris in France, the nearest star would be somewhere around Tokyo in far away Japan!

It surrounds the Solar System. The distance from the Sun to the Oort Cloud is between 10 and 20 million million kilometres!

## Beyond the Solar System

The Sun is a star, but looks much bigger and brighter than the other stars because it is much closer to us. The next nearest star to us is a quarter of a million times further away than the Sun. The Sun is just one of about 100 billion other stars that belong to the Milky Way **galaxy**. All the stars seen in the night sky belong to our galaxy. Some are hotter than the Sun, some cooler; some are bigger and some are smaller. Millions of other galaxies can be seen through powerful telescopes such as the Hubble Space Telescope. Some of these galaxies contain ten times as many stars as the Milky Way.

The Earth is a tiny and insignificant speck in the vastness of space.

## Try this – Scale model solar system

**You need:** copies or tracings of the planets opposite, a measuring tape and 6m of floor space

**What to do:** From the end of the floor measure out 5.8cm and put Mercury there. Venus should go 10.8cm from the end, the Earth at 15cm, Mars at 22.8cm, Jupiter at 77.8cm, Saturn at 143cm, Uranus at 287cm, Neptune at 448cm and Pluto at 594cm. Each centimetre represents 10 million kilometres of space.

# GLOSSARY

**asteroid** sometimes called a minor planet. Large rocky objects that orbit the Sun. The biggest, Ceres, is over 900 km across.

**atmosphere** layer of gases that surrounds the Earth

**atom** smallest part of a substance

**axis** imaginary line through the middle of an object around which it spins

**bacteria** simple forms of life found just about everywhere. They are too small to be seen without a microscope.

**block mountains** mountains that are formed by upward or downward movements along cracks in the Earth's crust

**celestial pole** one of two points in the sky about which the stars appear to turn when they are seen from the Earth

**climate** regular patterns of weather that are seen in a region over a number of years

**comet** frozen ball of gas and dust, like a dirty snowball, that travels round the Sun. When a comet comes close to the Sun some of the ice boils off to form a tail millions of kilometres long.

**core** hot, dense central part of the Earth

**corona** outer layer of hot gases surrounding the Sun

**crater** hole in the surface of an object in space caused by the impact of a meteorite

**crust** the outermost rocky layer of the Earth

**current** movement in a gas or liquid

**dome mountains** mountains formed by being pushed up from below by hot rock rising for the mantle

**eclipse** when the shadow of an object in space blocks the light from another object. A solar eclipse occurs when the Moon blocks the light from the Sun.

**epicentre** point on the Earth's surface that is directly above the focus of an earthquake

**erosion** wearing away of the Earth's surface by the forces of wind, water, ice and weather

**eruption** sudden explosion of gases, ash and molten rock from a volcano

**focus** point underground where the movement of the Earth that causes an earthquake takes place

**fold mountains** mountains formed when the Earth's surface is folded by the collision of massive sections of its crust

**fracture** crack or fault in rock

**fungi** types of living things, such as mushrooms, that get food by absorbing other living or decaying material

**galaxy** vast group of stars; there may be more than 100,000 million stars in a galaxy

**glacier** river of ice

**igneous** rock that has been formed when molten magma has cooled and solidified

**lava** molten magma that has flowed out on to the surface of the Earth

**lichen** a fungus and an alga growing together

**magma** molten rock inside the crust and mantle of the Earth

**mantle** hot dense layer of rock that lies beneath the Earth's crust

**metamorphic** rocks that have been changed beneath the ground by high pressures and temperatures but without them being melted

**meteor** dust from space that enters the Earth's atmosphere and burns up, causing a bright streak of light across the sky

**meteorite** rock from space that survives its journey through the atmosphere and hits the ground

**meteoroid** fragment of rock or dust travelling through space

**molten** made liquid by heat

**orbit** the path one object in space follows around another bigger object, for example the Earth around the Sun, or the Moon around the Earth

**planet** large object that orbits a star; nine planets orbit the Sun

**plate** one of the massive sections that the Earth's crust is divided into

**sediment** fragments of material from the weathering of rocks that are deposited by water or wind

**sedimentary** rocks that have been formed from sediments that are squeezed together under great pressure

**solstice** the period when there is the greatest difference between the lengths of day and night. The summer solstice is the time of the longest day, the winter solstice is the time of the longest night.

**time zone** region within which the same standard time is used

**tsunami** huge wave that travels across the ocean from the source of an earthquake

**Universe** all of space and everything in it

**weathering** the breaking down of rock by forces such as the weather, waves and ice

# INDEX